Street Racing

Peggy J. Parks
AR B.L.: 5.0
Points: 1.0   UG

Street Racing

by Peggy J. Parks

ERICKSON PRESS

Yankton, South Dakota

ERICKSON PRESS

© 2007 Erickson Press

For more information, contact
Erickson Press
329 Broadway
PO Box 33
Yankton, SD 57078

Or you can visit our Internet site at www.ericksonpress.com

LIBRARY OF CONGRESS CATALOGING-IN-PUBLICATION DATA

Parks, Peggy J., 1951–
    Street racing / Peggy J. Parks.
        p. cm.—(Ripped from the headlines)
    Includes bibliographical references and index.
    ISBN-13: 978-1-60217-019-3
    ISBN-10: 1-60217-019-3
    1. Traffic violations—United States. 2. Traffic accidents—United States. 3.
Automobile racing—United States. 4. Automobile racing—Accidents. I. Title.
    HV6424.P37 2007
    363.12'51—dc22
                                                            2007012764

Printed in the United States of America

Contents

"My Best Friend Was Killed Right Next to Me"

On April 21, 2006, Ian Morrill was driving his black, souped-up Honda Accord in Orange County, Florida. He was racing the driver of a sporty, white Subaru. They were going more than 100 miles per hour (161kph). All of a sudden the Subaru driver cut him off. Morrill smashed into the center highway divider. The impact was so violent that it ripped his car in half. He was thrown from the car and killed. He was only 21 years old. His best friend, Robert Taylor, was riding in Morrill's car. Taylor walked away from the accident with barely a scratch. He later posted his thoughts on an Internet message board: "I was involved in a car accident in which my best friend was killed right next to me. . . . Standing over a friend's body trying to help him stop bleeding when you realize that he will not make it home is something . . . [terrible]."[1]

High Speeds, High Risk

There are many sad stories like Morrill's. Thousands of street races take place every year. They are held in cities all over the United States. They are also held in Canada. Most drivers are young men in their late teens to early thirties. More and more young women are starting to street race, too.

How many kids take part, and how often, is not known. Street racing is an "underground sport." Races are planned in secret. Most of them happen late at night or very early in the morning. Police in many cities believe there are hundreds or even thousands of races each week. But they can only guess. There is no way for them to know for sure.

There are many reasons why street racing is deadly. One reason is that people drive their cars so fast. There was a high-speed race in June 2003 in Colorado Springs.

Police inspect the terrible aftermath of a fatal street racing crash in Riverside, California.

Jake Holmes was racing another car at about 130 miles per hour (209kph). He hit a dip in the road. His car flew through the air and crashed into a tree. Holmes did not die, but he was severely injured. He broke his pelvis. The muscles of his right leg were badly torn. He also suffered head injuries. He was in a coma for three weeks. He had to be in a wheelchair for the next six months.

Two years later, an accident in California was much worse. Three teenagers were racing in the city of Fremont. The speed limit was 35 miles per hour (56kph). They were going more than 80 miles per hour (129kph). The driver lost control of the car. He crashed into a tree. He and both passengers were killed.

Street races are also dangerous because they often take place on busy streets. They may last a few seconds or drag on for hours. Cars dangerously swerve in and out of traffic. Innocent people can be killed or injured. This happened in May 2005 in Gastonia, North Carolina. Five people were standing outside a Dairy Queen restaurant. A street racer lost control of his car and crashed into them. All the people were injured.

"It's a Rush"

The people who race on city streets know about the dangers. They also know that street racing is illegal. Sometimes those are the things that make them want to race. Racers like the thrill of driving very fast. They want to beat other cars. When they

Two cars travel at dangerously high speeds on wet pavement during an illegal street race in New Hampshire.

do, it is known as a kill. When they win more races, they can add cars to their "kill lists." The drivers like showing off in front of a crowd. They love pushing their cars, and their luck, to the limit. One racer named Zakk from Toronto, Canada, explains this kind of motivation: "I race because it's a rush. I don't do drugs or any of that garbage, so racing is my high for the moment."[2]

Walking Away

There are many people who feel like Zakk. They love racing and do not want to quit no matter what. Others have given up street racing for good.

They might have come close to getting hurt or dying. Or they might have just decided it was time to wise up.

Some people have stopped racing because it took the life of someone they cared about. This was the case with one of Ian Morrill's good friends. In an Internet forum, "DigMaster" talked about his friend. He said that after Morrill's death, street racing was no longer for him. "This is just a reminder for everyone to be safe and use very good judgment," he wrote. "It is hard to believe it is taking one of my closest friends death by racing to wake me up. I am for sure getting out of the street racing scene, and will keep it [strictly] on the track. I still can't believe this is happening, and would hate for this to happen to anyone else."[3]

Chapter 1

"It's Absolutely Insane"

On July 31, 2005, Stephen Buel was watching street races in Oakland, California. He was a journalist who was working on a report about street racing. Buel stood with a large group of people. They all watched as the cars lined up. The drivers took off and raced down the road. Then they returned to race again. Suddenly, Buel saw one of the cars speeding toward the crowd. He heard a sickening thud. He watched in horror as a body flew through the air. The body landed on the pavement near where he was standing. A teenage boy had been struck by the speeding car. As he lay still on the ground, blood pooled behind his head.

Buel was shocked because no one tried to help. Instead, people were shouting at each other to get out of there. One by one the drivers sped away in their cars. The rest of the people left, too. They were trying to escape in case the police showed up. Buel did not have a cell phone with him. He began yelling for someone to call 911. Everyone ignored him. Finally, one person made the call. Then he also ran away.

Buel was afraid. He was left alone with a young man he thought might be dying. He later wrote in a newspaper article: "How could they just leave like that? . . . It's hard . . . to escape the sad conclusion that some people value a fast car more than a human life."[4] The boy was fourteen-year-old Guillermo Estrada. He was badly hurt, but he did not die. It took him more than a year to recover from his injuries.

Problem Spots

Races like the one that almost killed Estrada happen often in Oakland. The city has had a problem with street racing for many years. In 2005 eleven people died from racing accidents. Police say the

During an illegal street race in Los Angeles, these young men watch dangerously close to the action.

Hot Cars

Most street racing cars are small imports. Hondas, Toyotas, Subarus, and Mitsubishis are some of the most popular cars. They handle well at high speeds and on curves. Imports are also easier to modify. Many parts on American cars must be welded on. With imports, the parts just bolt on and off. Drivers spend from $10,000 to $50,000 on high-performance parts. They buy new engine kits, exhaust systems, flashy wheels, racing tires, and spoilers. Sometimes they install systems that feed nitrous oxide (N_2O) into their engines. N_2O is a type of gas. It adds tremendous power and speed that can give drivers the edge in a race.

actual number of deaths was probably much higher. They do not know for sure how many street races are held. Because of that, they cannot always tell whether accident victims die because of racing or regular traffic crashes. Police officer Wayne Ziese explains: "How many of those calls that we get of high-speed aggressive drivers going down a freeway are actually two-way speed contests? It probably goes on every day. . . . It goes on every hour of every day."[5]

Salt Lake City, Utah, has problems with street races, too. Police say that the racing in Salt Lake is out of control. They say it puts people in the city in great danger. Reporters with KSL-TV wanted to see how bad the problem was. They did a secret investigation during the summer and fall of 2006. They planted hidden cameras so they could study racing activity. They saw young people trying to outsmart the police. The young people kept a close watch on the area. If they saw police officers, they used cell phones or headlight signals to warn their friends. Sheriff Scott Vanwagoner describes the situation in Salt Lake: "You can hear the engines revving, the tires spinning, the smoke rising from the tires. We've clocked them at 110 miles an hour on city streets. . . . It's absolutely insane, it frightens me to death."[6]

"They Have No Regard for Other People"

Street races in Salt Lake and other cities happen most often in the summer. That is when the weather is warm and the roads are dry. The drivers have different reasons for racing. Sometimes they just want to add cars to their kill lists. Or they may take bets and race for money. Occasionally, the stakes are much higher. Drivers may be so confident in their ability to win that they bet their cars. This is known as racing for pinks. The word *pinks* refers to the pink papers that show car ownership. Drivers risk losing cars in which they have

invested thousands of dollars. Kent Taylor
of the Ontario, Canada, provincial police
says that such high-stakes races are the
most dangerous of all: "For these people,
especially if they're racing for 'pinks,' there's sig-
nificant risk involved. They want to win, and it's
no holds barred. They have no regard for other
people on the roads."[7]

How Races Start

When people take part in street races, the races
can get started in different ways. Many are impromptu races. Those break out on the spur of
the moment. Someone who is driving notices a

Cheating Insurance

Modifying cars for street racing is a very expensive hobby. To get money for parts, drivers sometimes file false claims with insurance companies. Racers have been caught scraping their cars with keys or screwdrivers to get money for new paint jobs. They have slashed their cars' upholstery or smashed windows with baseball bats. Then they claim their cars were hit by vandals. They have even "stolen" their own tires or wheels. One Virginia man crashed his Ford Mustang in a street race. He knew his insurance policy would not cover damages caused by racing. So he claimed he had been in an accident. The company paid him $29,000. Then they did an investigation. They found out the truth and reported him for insurance fraud.

fancy car and challenges the driver to a race. He or she revs the car's engine to get the other driver's attention. Impromptu races are most common on freeways. That is where the speed limits are highest and traffic moves the fastest. Drivers cruise the freeways late at night. If they spot someone they want to race, they signal by flashing their lights.

Some street races are organized and planned ahead of time. Cars gather at a restaurant, gas station, parking lot, or other staging point. The racers challenge and taunt each other. They brag about their driving skills and how fast their cars can go. When it is time for the race to begin, it may start from a dig. That means the cars are at a dead stop and lined up side-by side. They take off when a flagger gives the sign. Other times the drivers may start from a roll. The cars are also lined up. But instead of being stopped, they are traveling together slowly down the road. When the flagger gives the signal, the drivers stomp on the gas pedal. A crowd watches the action, cheering for the drivers they want to win.

This teenage boy acts as a flagger to start an illegal drag race.

Extreme Racing

One type of organized race involves drifting. Drifting is considered an art as well as a sport to street racers. As drivers screech around curves, they make their cars drift, or skid sideways. Drifting can be very dangerous because the races are often held on narrow, curving mountain roads. *Sports Illustrated* writer Karl Taro Greenfeld describes this extreme form of racing:

> Riding with a drifter is like taking those split seconds before a car accident and extending them over a four-mile run. Your weight is repeatedly slammed from side to side as the vehicle careens at high speeds while the driver's feet and hands are in constant motion as he shifts, clutches, brakes and steers through thick clouds of clutch and tire smoke. If the window is open, bits of rubber and road will bounce off your face.[8]

Drifting races are booming in Southern California. The sport is also catching on in several other states. In the Los Angeles area, there are organized groups called drift crews. Two of the best-known crews are the Drift Monkeys and the Analog Assassins. Andrew Hateley is a member of the Analog Assassins. He began drifting soon after he learned to drive. Hateley is known as one of the best drifters in California.

Racers take part in a drifting exhibition in Southern California.

A Deadly Game

To people who are involved with street racing, the risk is part of the thrill. They drive at very high speeds. They put themselves in danger. They put other people in danger, too. They may speed on city streets or highways. Or they may drift around curving mountain roads. No

How Drifting Came to Be

In 1984 a Japanese race car driver was in a stock car race. His name was Keiichi Tsuchiya. He was coming in last, so he decided to show off for the crowd. Tsuchiya had learned some fancy tricks while driving on curving mountain roads. As he drove around the racetrack, he kept making his car slide sideways. The people in the crowd were cheering wildly. Someone videotaped the race. The tape was seen throughout Japan. Later a reporter asked Tsuchiya what he had been doing. He replied that he was "drifting." After that, the drifting craze caught on quickly in Japan. Later it spread to the United States and other countries.

matter what, they are taking part in a sport that is illegal and deadly. Kent Taylor offers a strong warning for them: "Street racing is not a joke and not a fun little hobby. You're risking lives. If you want to risk your own life, go parachute. Don't race on the street, taking other people's lives for your fun."[9]

Chapter 2

Street Racing Tragedies

When Joel Chan (not his real name) was eighteen, he street raced for the first time. Chan lived in the Alberni Valley area of British Columbia. His parents bought him an Acura Integra for his birthday. He fell in love with the car. He began to spend all his money and spare time working on it. About a month later he was in a street race. It was short, only from one traffic light to another. Even though the other car beat him, Chan was hooked. He vowed to work hard and make his Integra as powerful as it could be. Next time he intended to win.

Chan spent the next four months modifying his car. He spent thousands of dollars on new parts. Finally, he knew it was ready to race. He learned that street races were held every Friday night. He began to drive in all the races. Before long he was known as a street racing champion.

On a Friday night in July 2002, car engines were roaring in the valley. The races were about to begin. Chan's girlfriend, Stephanie, usually raced her own car. This night, though, she had agreed to be a flagger. She raised her hands above her head.

A young man works on his car. Street racers often add illegal changes to their cars.

Then she dropped them to give the signal. Without warning, a Ford Mustang slammed into her.

No one was looking in Stephanie's direction so they did not know what happened. The cars took off flying down the road. When the race ended, Chan and his friends spotted her. She was crumpled in a heap on the ground. They ran to help her, but it was too late. She was already dead. The car had hit her with such force that it instantly broke her neck.

Chan was filled with grief. He had planned to marry Stephanie, and he could not believe she was dead. Still, he felt he had to keep going. He had to get behind the wheel of his car again. The next Friday night he was back at the races. Even though his heart was not in it, he pushed himself hard. He won every single race.

"You Could Lose Everything"

By the time the races were over, it was raining. The roads had become wet and slippery. Chan was on his way home on the freeway. His friends were driving near him in separate cars. Suddenly, he saw the flashing lights of a police car in his rearview mirror. He was only driving a little over the speed limit. But instead of pulling over, he stomped on the gas pedal.

Chan drove faster and faster. Then he started skidding on the wet pavement. He lost control of

Ambulance personnel rush to the scene of a street race crash.

his car. He slammed into the wall of an underpass. The violent impact tore the car apart. The whole front end was almost twisted off. Chan could not move. He was pinned inside the car, screaming in pain. Hours passed before the paramedics could get him out. They rushed him to the hospital in an ambulance.

Chan was so badly injured that he almost died. His pelvis, both feet, and his left hand were shattered. He broke his right arm in three places. He broke both legs, five ribs, and his back. He also suffered severe head injuries. Doctors said he would never walk again. The accident left him paralyzed and in a wheelchair.

In May 2005 Chan talked about the accident with a friend and fellow racer. He said that even though street racing could be fun, it only led to tragedy and pain. "Please think of everyone including yourself," he begged, "because you don't know what is going to happen one night at the races or the roads. You could lose everything in the blink of an eye."[10]

Innocent Victims

Like Chan, Jonathan Hall also regrets street racing. On March 26, 2005, Hall raced another car in Gatlinburg, Tennessee. They were speeding on a curving road that led into the Great Smoky Mountains National Park. The race ended soon after it began. It caused the worst car accident ever recorded in the park's history.

The race began at a stoplight in town. Hall looked over and noticed a black Mustang beside him. He revved his engine to get the driver's attention. Steven Williams, the driver of the Mustang, revved his car's engine back. They were ready for the challenge. As soon as the light turned green, they took off. They continued to go

Motorcyclists often take part in illegal racing.

Two-Wheel Racing

Some of the most dangerous street races involve motorcycles. Motorcycle riders racing on highways or city streets have nothing to protect them if they crash. And just like cars, speeding motorcycles put innocent people in danger. In August 2006 three men were involved in a high-speed motorcycle race in Toronto, Canada. They were driving more than 150 miles per hour (240kph). Suddenly, one of them lost control of his bike. He slammed head-on into a car. The impact killed him instantly. A passenger in the car was also killed. Several other passengers were injured.

faster and faster. They chased each other up the narrow, winding mountain road. Their cars reached speeds of about 90 miles per hour (145kph).

After they had gone just over a mile, Williams's passenger shouted a warning. He had noticed a green Chrysler crossing the road up ahead. Williams screeched to a halt. He missed the car by mere inches. But Hall could not stop in time. His car slammed into the Chrysler. The impact made a thunderous crash. Shards of glass and pieces of metal flew all over the road. Five people

Great Smoky Mountains National Park in Tennessee was the scene of a car accident caused by illegal street racers.

who were inside the Chrysler were killed instantly. They were visitors from Virginia. They had been vacationing in Gatlinburg. Hall was arrested and taken to jail. Later he was sentenced to 22 years in prison. Williams received a lighter sentence, but he was sent to prison, too.

"Senseless Loss of Life"

A deadly crash in October 2002 also killed innocent victims. It happened on a Sunday evening just after sundown. Two drivers were racing down a busy street in San Diego. One of them was George Waller Jr. He was driving a souped-up Plymouth Barracuda. Waller was going about 90 miles per hour (145kph). He did not have his headlights on.

Shanna Jump was driving toward Waller from the opposite direction. Either she did not see his car in the darkness, or she misjudged its speed. She turned left in front of the speeding Barracuda. Waller slammed into her, causing a fiery crash that ripped her small, compact car apart. Jump and her boyfriend, Brian Hanson, were killed. Both were nineteen years old. Hanson's brother Michael was also in the car. He was seriously hurt in the accident. He suffered two broken legs and a broken pelvis. He also had severe brain injuries.

The following spring, Erik Pollock spoke at Waller's trial. He was a San Diego police officer

and the first person to arrive at the accident. He described the mangled car: "It was kind of like if you took a tin can and twisted it and bent it." When Pollock arrived at the scene, Jump was already dead. Brian Hanson was pinned inside the car. He was barely breathing and died soon afterward. As Pollock talked, he could not keep from crying. He spoke in a shaky voice on the witness stand: "What bothers me is just the senseless loss of life for something so stupid as drag racing."[11] Waller was found guilty of gross vehicular manslaughter in 2003. He will spend about seven years in prison.

A Fiery Death

In the early morning hours of March 30, 2005, Juan Carlos Cazares was driving his black Corvette. He was on a highway in Olmito, Texas. Cazares was racing a driver in a Ford Mustang. The cars were going more than 120 miles per hour (193kph). When Cazares rounded a curve, he lost control of his car. He spun around and flew across the median. He slammed into a concrete barrier. The crash caused the Corvette's gas tank to rupture. The car burst into flames. Firefighters put the blaze out within minutes. They could not save Cazares, however. He burned to death in the fire. Afterward, there was nothing left of the Corvette except the charred frame and engine.

Young Lives Wasted

Stories like these capture news headlines every day. Many of them have tragic endings. When people get involved in street races, they focus only on the fun they will have. They do it for the challenge, the thrill, the rush. If they thought about what could happen, maybe they would think twice before racing. Joel Chan, Jonathan Hall, and others like them wish they could have a second chance. Because of the mistakes they made, their lives will never be the same.

Chapter 3

Fueling the Craze

Car accidents are the number-one killer of young people aged fifteen to nineteen. Every year, between 5,000 and 6,000 teenagers are killed in car crashes. About 300,000 others are injured. As street racing has grown more popular, deaths related to traffic accidents have increased. Many law enforcement officials say there is a connection. One of these officials is Miami police officer Bill Schwartz. He expressed his frustration with the risks young people take: "Teenagers think drag racing is a movie. They don't understand that those people are stunt drivers, and that they can get killed."[12]

Speed on the Big Screen

Schwartz made his comments in June 2003. That was when the movie *2 Fast 2 Furious* opened in theaters. It was a movie about street racing. It was

Would building more quarter-mile racing strips reduce the number of illegal street races?

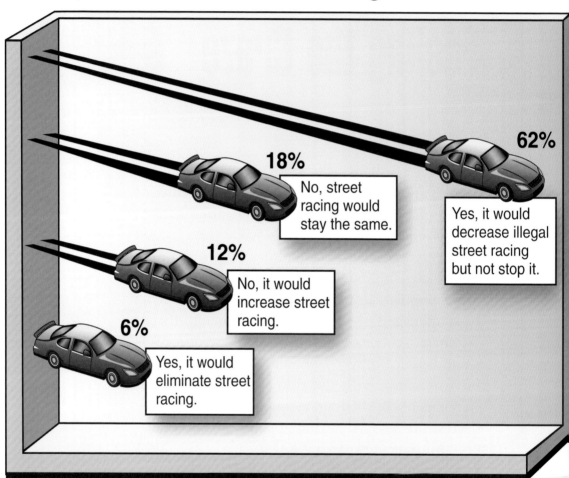

18%
No, street racing would stay the same.

62%
Yes, it would decrease illegal street racing but not stop it.

12%
No, it would increase street racing.

6%
Yes, it would eliminate street racing.

Source: MisterPoll, 2007.

a sequel to *The Fast and the Furious,* which had been released in 2001. That year, law enforcement officials started seeing a spike in car accident deaths. The National Highway Traffic Safety Administration studied the situation. They found that in 2001, the number of deadly crashes linked to street racing was 87 percent higher than in 2000.

When *2 Fast 2 Furious* came out, police again grew concerned. They feared that young people would try to copy the wild racing scenes in the film. That is what happened in San Francisco. In one night, police officers arrested six teenage drivers for racing. They were going more than 120 miles per hour (193kph). All of them had just seen *2 Fast 2 Furious*. The officers found the movie ticket stubs in their cars.

William Lacasse Jr. saw *2 Fast 2 Furious* when it first opened in Miami. He had driven his parents' Corvette to the theater. He was on his way home shortly after midnight. He stopped at a gas station. As he was pulling out onto the street, two Mitsubishi drivers noticed his fast car. They pulled up alongside him. They started flashing their hazard lights as a signal that they wanted to race.

A Father's Regret

Lacasse met their challenge. He floored the gas pedal and screeched out onto the road. Minutes later he lost control of the car. He slammed into a concrete utility pole. The violent collision blew the Corvette apart. It also snapped the pole in half. Lacasse was thrown from the car and killed. He was seventeen years old. His father was a Palm Beach County police officer. He said he had not known that his son was going to see the movie. If

A scene from 2 *Fast 2 Furious* shows young drivers standing in front of their racing cars.

he had been aware of it, he would never have let him drive the Corvette.

Behind the Virtual Wheel

Officer Lacasse believed his son was racing because of what he saw in the movie. Many other police officers worry about the same thing. In addition to movies, they are concerned about video games. Games such as Street Racing Syndicate and Midnight Club are very popular with young people. These video games are highly realistic. Players speed through traffic-clogged city streets in a virtual race car. In Midnight Club II, "drivers" race in Los Angeles, Paris, and Tokyo. The

Street Racing's Roots

When *The Fast and the Furious* first opened in 2001, street racing's popularity began to soar. But driving fast on city streets started long before that. In the late 1940s, more people could afford to buy cars than ever before. Young men who loved speed modified their cars to make them go faster. Drag racing became a popular sport. In 1951 some racing fans from Southern California formed the National Hot Rod Association. They organized racing events on airport runways and other makeshift tracks. Their goal was to make racing safer by getting it off public roads.

Dragsters speed down the track at an exhibition.

streets are crawling with cars, trucks, and buses. Pedestrians are walking on sidewalks and crossing streets. Police chase the speeding drivers in cars and helicopters. Unlike real life, there are no driving rules or laws in the game. Players just need to find the fastest possible route. Their object is to win the race without being caught.

No Reset Button

Another popular video game is Need for Speed. It also allows players to speed through crowded city streets. It features fiery car crashes that seem real. In January 2006 police found a copy of Need for Speed on the front seat of a Mercedes Benz. The car had just been in a deadly accident. The teenage driver was racing against another car through the streets of Toronto, Canada. Both cars were going about 90 miles per hour (145kph). The speed limit was only 30 miles per hour (48kph). A taxi driver tried to make a left turn. The Mercedes slammed into his taxicab. The impact caused the taxi to crash into a utility pole. The driver was killed instantly. The boy who caused the accident walked away with barely a scratch.

Police detective Paul Lobsinger investigated the accident. He talked about the connection between video games and street racing. "A game is a game," he said. "And when you get behind the wheel of a car it's not a game anymore. And when something tragic happens in a huge crash with a lot of smoke, there is no reset button. You can't start over with a

Car racing games such as this one for an Xbox 360 are very realistic.

Fantasy and Reality

The Fast and the Furious: Tokyo Drift is the latest movie about street racing. It was shot in Japan. It features souped-up cars drifting around the curves of city streets. The film makes drifting look easy. But the cars were driven by professional stunt drivers. They are some of the top drifters in the world. They wore protective harnesses when they drove. Their cars had steel cages to protect them in case of rollovers. Before drifting scenes were filmed, the roads were closed to the public. Medical crews were nearby in case anyone was injured. Over the course of making the movie, more than a hundred cars were destroyed.

new car and a new life." Lobsinger added, however, that video games should not be blamed for the crash. "There is a small percentage who have difficulty separating reality and simulation, or fantasy. This wasn't the game's fault. There are millions who play this game and don't go out and do this."[13] Lobsinger also said that people naturally make such connections when accidents happen.

Street Racing on the Web

Some police officers share Lobsinger's viewpoint. Others do not. Those who disagree think that movies and video games are partly responsible for accidents caused by street racing. There is one thing that police officers often do agree on. They think that movies and games help to fuel the street racing craze. The same is true of the Internet. Many people have created street racing Web sites. They post stories, photographs, race results, and other information. Free services such as MySpace and Blogger.com host the sites for free.

Racing fans also share videos with each other. Video cameras are common at street races. Drivers love to show off for the camera. After a race, they can post their videos on the Web. Then they can let people all over the world see their racing skills.

YouTube is a very popular video-sharing site. As of April 2007, there were nearly 7,100

Illegal street racers show off on Internet video-sharing sites like YouTube.

street racing videos on YouTube. One showed a young driver from England. He was traveling more than 115 miles per hour (185kph). As he flew around a corner, he almost crashed into another car. A different video showed a teenager speeding toward a dangerous bend in the road. He was laughing like it was a joke. Many videos on YouTube show real-life street racing accidents. One of them showed a car that crashed. Flames were shooting out of its rear end. People at the scene were running around and yelling in panic.

Street racing fans also share experiences on Internet discussion boards. They talk about racing on the street and on the track. They discuss their cars and how they have modified them. They talk about accidents they have seen or been involved

YouTube Oops!

During the summer of 2006, there was a street race in Winnipeg, Canada. The race was videotaped. The drivers later posted a video clip on YouTube. It showed two cars traveling at high speeds through city streets. It was entitled "Racing a Turbo Civic." Thousands of people saw it, including two police officers. They caught a glimpse of one driver's face and license plate. They also saw the racers' names at the end of the video. The officers tracked the drivers down. They were arrested and charged with reckless driving.

Street racers and fans gather at a legal track on the Barona Indian Reservation in San Diego County, California.

in. They share problems they have had with police. They plan and announce upcoming races. Sometimes they get into arguments. On the Web site ModdedMustangs.com, one person lashed out at someone who was in favor of illegal racing: "[W]hen someone innocent who is following the traffic laws perfectly gets killed by someone ILLEGALLY street racing it is a tragedy . . . if you think otherwise then you are just plain stupid."[14]

The Questions Linger

Movies, video games, and the Web help fuel the street racing craze. No one can say for sure they are to blame when laws are broken or accidents happen. Many people are convinced there is a connection. Others say that there is not. They say that racers are responsible for their own actions and the blame belongs to them. The truth probably falls somewhere in the middle.

Chapter 4

Fighting Back

Police officers get tired of fighting the battle against street racing. They are viewed as the bad guys when they move in and try to break up races. Oakland police captain David Kozicki explains how frustrating this can be: "We get the same arguments about street racing. . . . You know, 'These are people just having fun; they're not hurting anybody; they just want to show off their car.' And yet people end up dead."[15]

"All These People Start Running"

It is a huge challenge for police to catch racers in the act. Racers monitor police activity with scanners. If they hear anything that makes them suspicious, they quickly spread the word. By the time the officers get there, the crowd has broken up. There can also be problems if police do arrive while a race is going on. The second people spot

Police make a surprise visit to an illegal street race.

them, they will do anything to get away. This can create a situation that is even more dangerous than the race itself. Kozicki explains: "When law enforcement swoops in, all these people start running in one direction or another."[16] That sort of panic can result in risky high-speed chases.

Nowhere to Hide

Police try to avoid such chases because they are so dangerous. Instead, they look for other ways to catch street racers. This kind of smart thinking led to a successful raid in March 2004. It happened in the town of Tracy, California. The operation had been planned for months. Police from three cities, the county, and the state took part. Undercover officers began to attend races and videotape them. The group studied the tapes. They identified cars that they wanted to get off the street.

Enhanced Driver's Ed

In 2001 an organization called Racers Against Street Racing (RASR) was formed in California. The group's goal was to teach high school students about the dangers of street racing. RASR members also told the kids about legal races at tracks. According to the group's Web site, "RASR and industry professionals are working to spread the word and make it 'cool' to get off the streets and onto the track." Today the RASR's program is being used in driver's education classrooms around the country.

Racers Against Street Racing, "About RASR." www.enjoythedrive.com/content/?id=31665.

On the night the raid was to take place, the racers started gathering around midnight. The undercover officers mingled with the group. At least a thousand people had come to watch the races. There were more than 300 cars. About 1:00 AM, police moved in. In a blaze of flashing lights, dozens of police cars surrounded the area. Officer Robert Rickman explains what happened next: "It was like hitting a beehive with a stick. You saw people running around, backing up, driving all across the parking lot trying to find an escape, but there wasn't any."[17] By the end of the night, police had arrested more than a dozen people. They also seized nearly 60 cars.

Crime Does Not Pay

In the past, such arrests did little to stop street racers. They just paid their fines and went right back to racing. Now that is starting to change. States are getting tougher on the people who take part. One state that has passed strict laws is Texas. People involved in street racing can go to jail for up to six months. Also, drivers and passengers can be fined $2,000. Even people who watch races can be arrested and fined $500.

California has also taken a tough approach to street racing. In September 2006 new laws were passed. They made the penalties harsher than ever before. As in Texas, drivers in California can be

Illegal Street Racing Statistics

Motor vehicle accidents are the leading cause of death for people between the ages of 16 and 20.

Forty-nine people are injured out of every 1,000 who participate in illegal street racing.

In 2001 the number of fatal crashes in the United States resulting from illegal street racing jumped by 87%. That was the year *The Fast and the Furious* was released into theaters.

More than 800 citations for illegal street racing were issued in California in 2001. In Florida 7,216 citations were issued for racing on the highway the same year.

In 2003 nearly 40% of male drivers 15 to 20 years old involved in driving accidents were speeding.

Illegal street racing caused more than 500 accidents and 40 deaths in California between 2001 and 2005.

In San Diego, California, 16 deaths and 31 serious injuries were directly related to illegal street race crashes in 2002.

San Diego, California, became the first city to pass an ordinance making it a crime to attend an illegal street race.

Sources: National Highway Traffic Safety Administration; California Department of Motor Vehicles; National Hot Rod Association.

slapped with large fines. They can also be made to serve time in jail or prison.

In addition to state laws, many California cities have passed their own laws and ordinances. San Diego is one of them. The city has had problems with street racing for years. Starting in 2001 the problem began to grow worse. On Friday and Saturday nights, a thousand or more cars raced at six sites. Thousands of people gathered to watch. According to public health officials, 16 people were killed in street races during 2002. Another 31 people were injured.

The following year San Diego began to crack down on street racing. Drivers and people in the crowd were arrested and jailed. Their cars were towed away by police. To get them back, owners had to pay hundreds of dollars. Drivers who still refused to stop racing faced even tougher punishment. After two convictions, they lost their cars for good. San Diego police detective Greg Sloan says these strict laws have made a difference. "We'll arrest them, fine them, take their licenses, and throw them in jail. They'll get on the Internet and tell other racers, 'This isn't just a speeding ticket anymore. It's going to cost me 10 grand.' And that doesn't take into account the seven years of bad luck on their car insurance."[18]

Goodbye Cars

San Diego police constantly keep an eye on the city's streets. They watch for cars that look and sound like

RaceLegal

Stephen Bender, a retired public health professor, watched street racing become a serious problem in San Diego. He decided to do something about it. Bender created a way for young people to race without being on the streets. He formed an organization called RaceLegal. It sponsored Friday night races in the parking lot of a large San Diego stadium. Bender's idea caught on. RaceLegal races are now held in cities all over the United States and Canada.

Drivers line up for a legal drag race in New Hampshire.

An open trunk reveals the extreme changes made to this street race car.

they are used for street racing. Officers are trained to spot vehicles with extreme modifications. They cruise the streets looking for certain exhaust systems, large spoilers, and other telltale features. Many of these cars are not street legal. When officers are suspicious of a car, they pull the driver over. They inspect the car to see if it has illegal modifications. If so, the driver is arrested and the car is taken away.

If officers find that a car has been modified with stolen parts, the result is much worse. In the first nine months of 2006, almost 10,000 cars were stolen in San Diego. Many were import cars typically used for street racing. When police find cars that have stolen motors or transmissions, they seek a court order to have the cars destroyed. Most end up being sent to a giant machine known as the

Smile for the Camera

Police in San Diego started a program called Drag Net. It is the country's only law enforcement unit devoted to stopping street racing. A team of undercover officers works for the Drag Net unit. They attend street races and videotape them. Then they go to racers' homes with the tapes. They confront the racers and their parents face-to-face. Sometimes they take news reporters along. As drivers are handcuffed and taken away by the police, reporters are on the scene to film it for the evening news.

Police in Los Angeles can crush the cars of illegal street racers after just a single offense.

crusher. Cars worth tens of thousands of dollars are flattened into hunks of scrap metal.

The city of Los Angeles goes even further than that. Police officers can take a racer's car away after just one offense. The car can be towed to a junkyard and smashed. One Los Angeles law enforcement official explained: "To racers, their cars are everything. If you crush them, that sends a powerful message."[19]

Off the Streets, On the Track

Police know that even the toughest laws cannot stop all racing. Too many people want to experience the thrill of driving fast. So instead of trying to stop them, some cities hold supervised races. The drivers register and pay an entry fee. They can race their cars on a track in front of a crowd of racing fans. They get the same thrills and cheers from the crowd. But unlike street racing, what these drivers are doing is legal. The races are also safer because they are supervised. So they do not put innocent people in danger.

Gunnar Nettleship is a former street racer. He says he used to do "stupid, dangerous things." He often raced at high speeds through the streets of Los Angeles. When he was in his early twenties, he had a scary experience. He was speeding around a sharp curve and almost

Racers drive a track in Minnesota. Legal racing is growing in popularity across the country.

flew off the side of a mountain. That experience terrified him. Now Nettleship races only on legal tracks. "I've learned that no matter how good a driver you think you are," he says, "somebody else can make the mistake that gets you killed. So why risk your life? I drive on the street as safely as I can, and when I want to drive hard and fast, I go to the track."[20] Police officers everywhere hope that more young people make the same wise decision.

Notes

Introduction: "My Best Friend Was Killed Right Next to Me"

1. Robert Taylor, "Fatal Car Accident," HHD Forums, April 26, 2006. www.hiphop-direc tory.com/forums/archive/index.php/t-13552. html.
2. Quoted in Kevin Ketchen, "Illegal Street Racing: The Real World of the Fast & the Furious," *Faze Magazine*, Spring 2002. www. fazeteen.com/spring2002/streetracing.htm.
3. DigMaster, "R.I.P.—Ian Morrill 4/21/06," South Florida Racing.com. www.southflori daracing.com/forums/showthread.php?t=372 62.

Chapter 1: "It's Absolutely Insane"

4. Stephen Buel, "The Quick and the Dead," *East Bay Express*, July 26, 2006. www.eastbay express.com/Issues/2006-07-26/news/feature. html.
5. Quoted in Buel, "The Quick and the Dead."

6. Quoted in Debbie Dujanovic, "Street Racing: An Investigative Report," KSL-TV News, February 3, 2005. http://tv.ksl.com/index.php?sid=148595&nid=5.

7. Quoted in CBC News Online, "Street Racing: Too Fast, Too Furious," June 15, 2006. www.cbc.ca/news/background/crime/street-racing.html.

8. Karl Taro Greenfeld, "Catch the Drift," *Sports Illustrated*, April 28, 2006. http://sportsillustrated.cnn.com/2006/writers/the_bonus/04/26/drifting/index.html.

9. Quoted in CBC News Online, "Street Racing."

Chapter 2: Street Racing Tragedies

10. Quoted in A.J. Michelson, "Confessions of a Street Racer," *Racer's Edge*, May 28, 2005. www.alberni.ca/modules/soapbox/article.php?articleID=25.

11. Quoted in Harriet Ryan, "Witnesses Recount Gruesome Drag Racing Accident," Court TV News, May 14, 2003. www.courttv.com/trials/dragrace/050803_ctv.html.

Chapter 3: Fueling the Craze

12. Quoted in Associated Press, "Drag Race Deaths, Fast Film Linked," CBS News, June

26, 2003. www.cbsnews.com/stories/2003/ 06/26/entertainment/main560612.shtml.

13. Quoted in Tim Surette, "NFS Found in Fatal Drag-Racing Car Crash," GameSpot.com, January 26, 2006. www.gamespot.com/ps2/ driving/needforspeedmostwanted/news.html? sid=6143195.

14. Quoted in ModdedMustangs.com, Forums, "Street Racing Tragedies," September 12, 2006. www.moddedmustangs.com/forums/ street-racing-tragedies-vt1512.html.

Chapter 4: Fighting Back

15. Quoted in Buel, "The Quick and the Dead."
16. Quoted in Buel, "The Quick and the Dead."
17. Quoted in Buel, "The Quick and the Dead."
18. Quoted in John Lehrer, "A Deadly Game," *Westways Magazine*, Automobile Club of Southern California, May/June 2005. www.aaa-calif.com/westways/0505/features/ deadlygame. aspx.
19. Quoted in Carol Marin, "The Deadly World of Street Racing: It's Exciting, It Draws Crowds—and It's Illegal, Say Cops Out to Stop It," *Chicago Sun-Times*, July 17, 2006, p. 8.
20. Quoted in Lehrer, "A Deadly Game."

Glossary

drifting: Sliding one's car sideways through tight turns.

flagger: The person who signals the start of a race.

from a dig: Starting a race from a dead stop.

from a roll: Starting a race while cars are lined up and traveling slowly down the road.

impromptu races: Races that happen spontaneously, such as one driver challenging another at a stoplight.

kill: A racing victory.

kill list: The list of cars that a driver has beaten in races.

nitrous oxide (N_2O): A gas that is sometimes used to make car engines more powerful.

pinks: Ownership papers of a car.

staging point: The place where a race begins, such as a parking lot or alley.

Bibliography

Books

Tom Benford, *The Street Rod.* St. Paul, MN: MBI Publishing, 2004. Readers learn about how racecars have changed from the hot rods of yesterday to the super-modified cars of today.

National Hot Rod Association, *The Fast Lane: The History of NHRA Drag Racing.* New York: Regan Books, 2001. Lots of colorful pictures help tell the story of the NHRA's 50-year history of drag racing.

Magazines and Newspapers

Linda Davis, "Teen Has a Way with Wheels," *Contra Costa Times,* July 10, 2003. The story of Liz Miles, a California teenager who rebuilds her own engines and loves to race cars on legal racetracks.

Eric C. Evarts, "Ride the Fastest Machines on Earth," *Christian Science Monitor,* June 23, 2004. An interesting article about drag racing, including a brief history of the sport.

Dennis Jay, "Deadly Street Racing Activity Fuels Latest Variety of Insurance Fraud," *National*

Underwriter Property & Casualty-Risk & Bene-fits Management, October 3, 2005. A story about the different ways street race drivers are cheating insurance companies in order to buy parts for their expensive cars.

Internet Sources

John Lehrer, "A Deadly Game," Automobile Club of Southern California, *Westways Magazine*, May/June 2005. www.aaa-calif.com/westways/0505/features/deadlygame.aspx. An informative article about street racing in the past and the present, including why it is so dangerous, how racers try to outsmart law enforcement, and how the police are working to stop it.

Ryan Stevens, "Drifting Explained!" *SRO Magazine*, September 19, 2006. www.sromagazine.com/home.php?op=go&id=350. A member of Japan's Velocity Racing Team wrote this article, which provides a good explanation of drifting.

Web Sites

Answerbag: Street Racing (www.answerbag.com/c_view/2005). This is a forum where people can ask questions about street racing and get straight answers from people who know about the subject.

National Hot Rod Association (NHRA) Street Legal (www.nhra.com/streetlegal). Includes information about legal drag racing tracks, advice from professional race car drivers about right and wrong ways to race, fun facts, and "True Story" articles such as "Confessions of a Former Street Racer."

RaceLegal.com (www.racelegal.com). Discusses the history behind the RaceLegal organization, upcoming racing events, results of races held, a photo gallery, and racer profiles.

Racers Against Street Racing (RASR) (www. rasr.info). The official site of RASR, a group that is devoted to getting racing off the street and onto legal tracks. One feature of this site is a list of RASR racetracks grouped by state.

Index

Picture Credits

Cover: © John Green/Icon SMI/Corbis

AP Photo/Brainerd Dispatch/Steve Kohls, 33
AP Photo/Frank Wiese, 10, 15
AP Photo/Jim Cole, 47
AP Photo/Paul Sakuma, 35
AP Photo/St. Cloud Times, Jason Wachter, 51
© Jeff Paris, 39
© Jerry Arcieri/Corbis, 37
© John Green/Icon SMI/Corbis, 17
Jupiterimages Unlimited/Ablestock, 24
Jupiterimages Unlimited/Comstock, 22, 27
Jupiterimages Unlimited/Photos.com, 48, 50
Jupiterimages Unlimited/ThinkStock, 20, 42
Maury Aaseng, 30, 45
© Rick Friedman/Corbis, 7, 13
© Steven K. Doi/ZUMA/Corbis, 5
Universal/The Kobal Collection/Reed, Eli, 32
© W. Cody/Corbis, 25

About the Author

Peggy J. Parks holds a bachelor of science degree from Aquinas College in Grand Rapids, Michigan, where she graduated magna cum laude. She is a freelance author who has written more than 50 nonfiction books for children and young adults. Parks lives in Muskegon, Michigan, a town that she says inspires her writing because of its location on the shores of Lake Michigan.